Maths BOOSTER

Year 3

Peter Patilla

Teachers' notes and answers may be viewed and downloaded free of charge from: **www.letts-education.com/mathsboosters**

First published 2001

Letts Educational, The Chiswick Centre, 414 Chiswick High Road, London W4 5TF
Telephone: (020) 8996 3333
Fax: (020) 8742 8390
www.letts-education.com

Text: © Peter Patilla

Author: Peter Patilla

Series project editor: Nancy Terry

Series designer: Ken Vail Graphic Design, Cambridge

Illustrations: Sylvie Poggio Artists Agency (Lisa Williams)

All rights reserved. No part of this publication may be reproduced, stored in a retrieval system, or transmitted, in any form or by any means electronic, mechanical, photocopying, recording or otherwise, without the prior permission of Letts Educational.

British Library Cataloguing in Publication Data
A CIP record for this book is available from the British Library.

ISBN 1840855878

Printed in the UK

Reprographics by PDQ

Letts Educational, a division of Granada learning Ltd.
Part of the Granada Media Group.

Maths BOOSTER
Year 3

Contents

Place value 4	Missing digits 27
Positions 5	Mental differences 28
Money .6	Adding nines 29
Measurements 7	Adding 2-digit numbers 30
Number patterns 8	Subtracting nines 31
Fractions of shapes 9	Subtracting 2-digit numbers 32
Fractions of numbers 10	Addition HTU 33
Rounding to 10 11	Subtraction HTU 34
Rounding to 100 12	Division 1 35
Odds and evens 13	Division 2 36
Fractions 14	Remainders 1 37
Rounding measures and money . .15	Remainders 2 38
Ordering numbers 16	Halving 39
Multiples 17	Money problems 2 40
Halfway 18	Measurement problems 2 41
Addition and subtraction TU 19	Tens and hundreds 42
Complements 20	Multiplication TU 43
Calculation words 21	Calculation links 44
Money problems 1 22	Triples .45
Measurement problems 1 23	Shape knowledge 1 46
Multiplication tables 24	Shape knowledge 2 47
Doubling 25	Brainbox 48
Mental problems 26	

Place value

Warm up

1. What is the 3 worth in 738?
   a 3   b 30   c 300

2. What is the missing number in this calculation?
   367 = 300 + ☐ + 7
   a 6   b 60   c 600

3. Which number is 100 more than 375?
   a 385   b 475   c 1375

4. Which is the largest number that can be made from any three of these digits?
   3   7   6   2
   a 673   b 723   c 763

A

Look at the coloured digit in each pair of numbers.
Write the difference in value between the coloured digits.

1. 375   726   difference =
2. 875   428   difference =
3. 154   773   difference =
4. 703   350   difference =
5. 903   623   difference =
6. 712   368   difference =

To find the **difference**, you subtract. The **difference** between 600 and 60 is 540.

B

Write the number that is 1 more than each of these.

2578 — These are **thousands**

1 299   3 999   5 5099   7 9099   9 9009
2 579   4 2089   6 4999   8 9909   10 9089

C

Look at the number 2056.

Change the order of the figures to make the biggest number possible.

4

Positions

Warm up
Which number is each arrow pointing to?

1. 0 —→— 100   a 50   b 60   c 70
2. 0 —→— 100   a 68   b 72   c 78
3. 0 —→— 100   a 15   b 25   c 55
4. 0 —→— 1000 a 55   b 505 c 250
5. 0 —→— 1000 a 40   b 500 c 400
6. 0 —→— 1000 a 71   b 710 c 790

A
Write the number each arrow is pointing to.

1. A, B on 0–200 scale
2. C, D on 0–50 scale
3. E, F on 5000–6000 scale
4. G, H on 0–500 scale
5. I, J on 100–200 scale

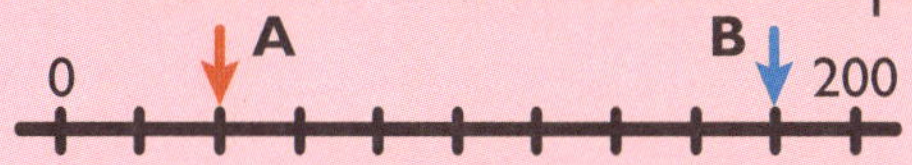

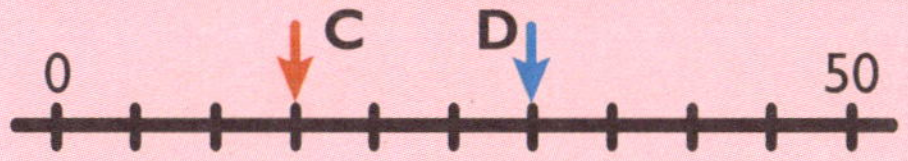

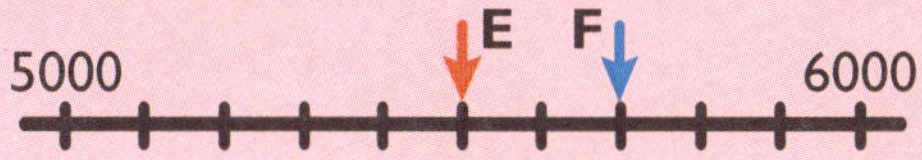

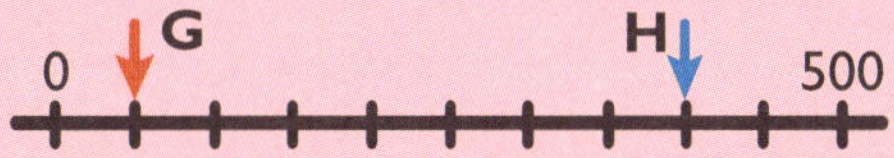

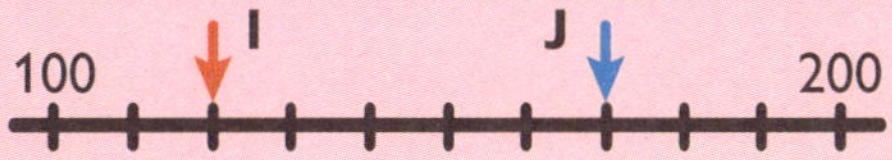

Look at the end numbers. Work out what each division mark is worth.

B
What is the reading on each of these spring balances?

1. (grams, scale to 500)
2. (grams, scale to 1000)

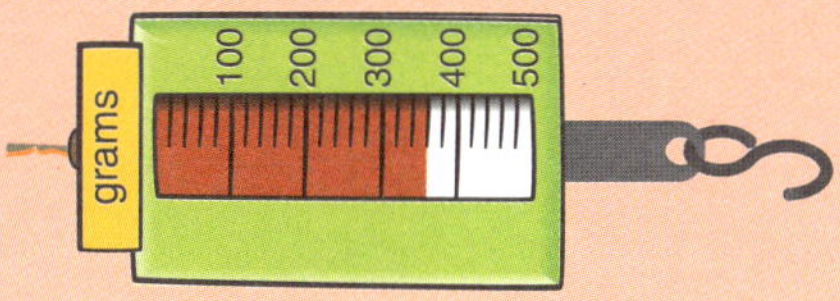

You should work out what each mark stands for.

C
How much liquid is in the jug?

200 ml
500 ml
800 ml

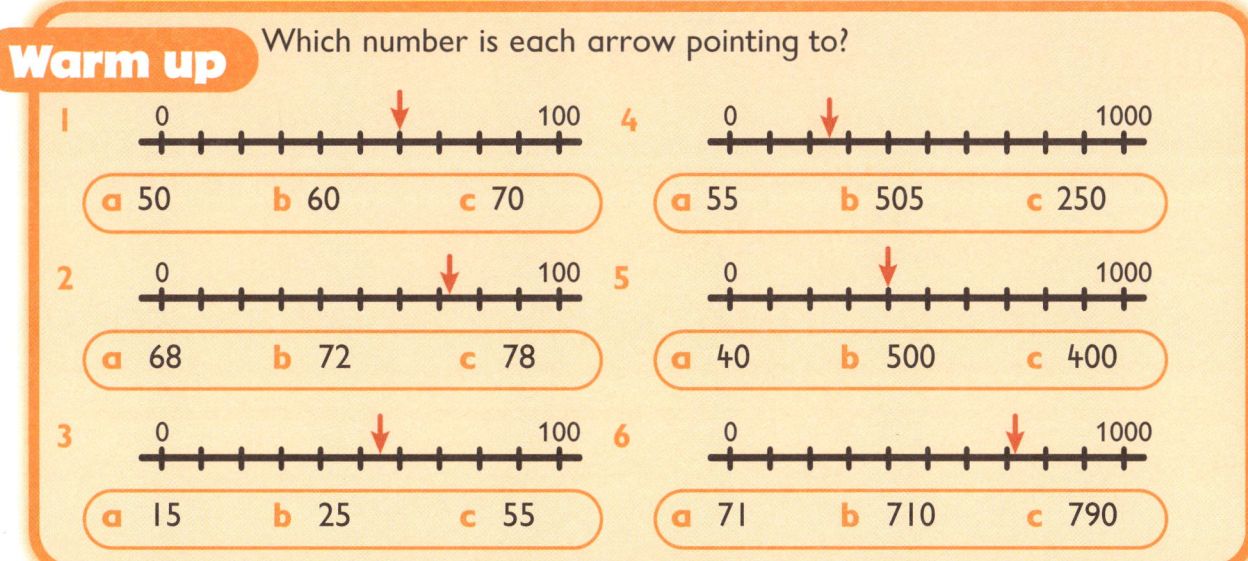

Money

Warm up

1. Change £1.35 to pennies.
   a 13   b 35   c 135

2. Change £4.35 to pennies.
   a 35   b 45   c 435

3. Change 175p to pounds.
   a £1.75   b £17.50   c £175

4. Change 250p to pounds.
   a £25   b £2.05   c £2.50

A

Change each of these into pounds.

1. 25p =
2. 8p =
3. 104p =
4. 280p =
5. 300p =
6. 407p =
7. 610p =
8. 1200p =
9. 1550p =
10. 2500p =

Change each of these into pennies.

1. £0.45
2. £1.08
3. £4
4. £12.50
5. £17.00
6. £0.06
7. £2.90
8. £10
9. £15.25
10. £20

The point separates the pounds from the pennies, and there are always two numbers after the point.

B

Write how much these are altogether in pounds.

1. six 10p coins and five 1p coins
2. five 20p coins and three 5p coins
3. six £1 coins and four 10p coins
4. five £2 coins and four 2p coins
5. ten £2 coins and ten 5p coins
6. ten 10p coins and three 2p coins
7. ten £1 coins and six 1p coins
8. eight £1 coins and five 5p coins
9. three £2 coins and two 1p coins
10. five £2 coins and three 20p coins

C

Write the amounts that are halfway between each of these.

1. £5 and £6
2. £2 and £2.50
3. £4.50 and £5

Measurements

Warm up

1. What is 3 metres in centimetres?
   a 30 cm   b 300 cm   c 3000 cm

2. What is 5 kilograms in grams?
   a 50 g   b 500 g   c 5000 g

3. What is 6 litres in millilitres?
   a 60 mℓ   b 600 mℓ   c 6000 mℓ

4. What is 700 cm in metres?
   a 0.7 m   b 7 m   c 70 m

5. What is 4000 g in kilograms?
   a 4 kg   b 40 kg   c 400 kg

6. What is 2000 mℓ in litres?
   a 2 ℓ   b 20 ℓ   c 200 ℓ

A

Change each of these into centimetres.

1. 1.70 m
2. 2.05 m
3. 1.75 m
4. 5.13 m
5. 2.35 m
6. 3.33 m
7. 4.25 m
8. 8.82 m

Change each of these into metres.

1. 160 cm
2. 775 cm
3. 611 cm
4. 470 cm
5. 302 cm
6. 599 cm
7. 375 cm
8. 409 cm

The point separates the whole metres from the centimetres:
2.40 m = 2 metres 40 cm

B

Write these using the point between metres and centimetres.

1. two and a half metres
2. six and a half metres
3. three and a half metres
4. ten and a half metres

Now write these, also using the point.

5. one and a half kilograms
6. two and a half litres
7. six and a half kilograms
8. nine and a half litres

Look at these:
Half a metre = 0.5 m or 0.50 m
Half a kilogram = 0.5 kg
Half a litre = 0.5 ℓ

C

Write =, < or > in the boxes to make the statements true.

350 cm ☐ 3.05 m $2\frac{1}{2}$ m ☐ 2.5 m

Number patterns

Warm up Which numbers should be in the coloured boxes?

1. | | | | 54 | 55 | 56 | 57 | | |

   a 58   b 59   c 60   d 61

2. | | | | 77 | 76 | 75 | 74 | | |

   a 80   b 81   c 82   d 83

3. | | | | 123 | 133 | 143 | 153 | | |

   a 183   b 193   c 203   d 213

4. | | | | 656 | 756 | 856 | 956 | | |

   a 756   b 356   c 256   d 156

A Copy and complete these number patterns.

1 13 18 23 ☐ 33 38 ☐ 48

2 90 ☐ 82 78 74 ☐ 66 62

3 101 ☐ 107 ☐ 113 116 119 ☐

4 34 45 ☐ 67 78 89 100 ☐

5 ☐ ☐ 19 25 31 ☐ 43 49

6 300 275 250 ☐ 200 ☐ ☐ 125

Find the difference between next-door numbers. This may help to spot the patterns.

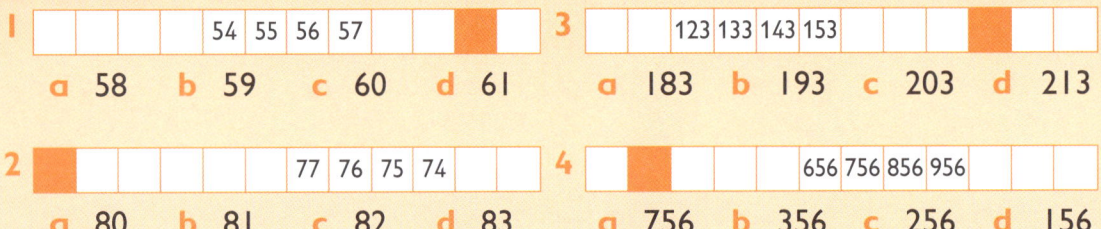

B

1 What is the fifth multiple of 2?

2 What is the fourth multiple of 10?

3 What is the third multiple of 4?

4 Which multiple of 2 comes between 32 and 36?

5 What is the sixth multiple of 5?

6 What is the sixth multiple of 3?

7 Which multiple of 5 comes between 55 and 65?

8 Which multiple of 10 comes between 31 and 41?

You need to know what multiples are. If you are not sure, try to find out.

C Look at this pattern of numbers. Write the missing number.

51 44 37 ☐ 23 16

Fractions of shapes

Warm up   What fraction has been eaten?

1    3

   a $\frac{1}{4}$ b $\frac{1}{2}$ c $\frac{3}{4}$ a $\frac{1}{4}$ b $\frac{1}{2}$ c $\frac{3}{4}$

2    4

   a $\frac{1}{3}$ b $\frac{1}{2}$ c $\frac{2}{3}$ a $\frac{1}{7}$ b $\frac{1}{8}$ c $\frac{1}{6}$

A Write which of these has one-third coloured.

A  B  C  D 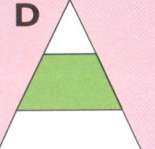 E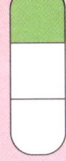

Check whether each part is exactly the same size.

B Write which of these has one-quarter coloured.

A 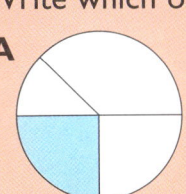 B  C 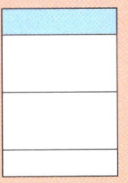 D 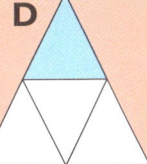 E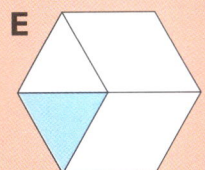

Look at the whole, then look at the coloured part. Decide whether it is a quarter.

C Write the fraction that has been coloured. Do not use tenths!

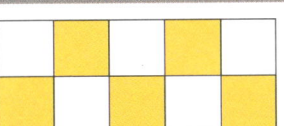

9

Fractions of numbers

Warm up What fraction has been coloured?

1

    a $\frac{1}{4}$ b $\frac{1}{3}$ c $\frac{2}{3}$

3

    a $\frac{1}{4}$ b $\frac{1}{3}$ c $\frac{2}{3}$

2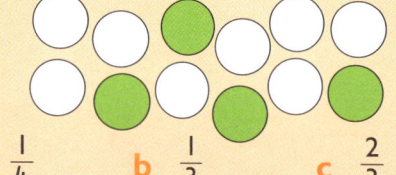

    a $\frac{1}{4}$ b $\frac{1}{3}$ c $\frac{2}{3}$

4

    a $\frac{1}{9}$ b $\frac{1}{2}$ c $\frac{3}{4}$

A

Copy the tables.
Write the numbers that leave the function machine.

In	3	7	11	19	27
Out					

In	5	9	15	12	29
Out					

*When you halve **odd numbers**, they always have a half in the answer.*

B

Find three-quarters of the following.

1 16   3 24
2 20   4 40

Find two-thirds of the following.

5 12   7 18
6 24   8 30

To find $\frac{3}{4}$, work out $\frac{1}{4}$ first.
To find $\frac{2}{3}$, work out $\frac{1}{3}$ first.

C

What fraction of dots has been coloured?
Write the fraction in two ways.

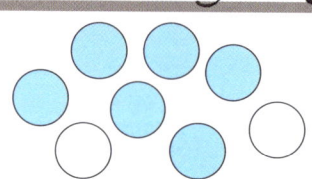

10

Rounding to 10

Warm up

Round each number to the nearest 10.

1. 56
   - a 50 b 55 c 60

2. 99
   - a 90 b 95 c 100

3. 55
   - a 50 b 55 c 60

4. 44
   - a 40 b 45 c 50

5. 81
   - a 80 b 85 c 90

6. 92
   - a 90 b 95 c 100

A

Round each of these to the nearest 10.

1. 458
2. 206
3. 379
4. 582
5. 704
6. 431
7. 824
8. 605
9. 667

Look at the units part of the number. If it is 5 or more, you round up to the next 10.

B

Round each of these to the nearest 10.

Sometimes when you round to the nearest 10, it pushes the number on into the next 100.
*So **396 rounds up to 400.***

1. 699
2. 595
3. 996
4. 794
5. 893
6. 993
7. 497
8. 496
9. 999

C

What must be added to each number to round it up to the next 10?

125   406   892   651

Rounding to 100

Warm up Round each number to the nearest 100.

1. 256
   a. 200 b. 300 c. 500

2. 726
   a. 600 b. 700 c. 800

3. 391
   a. 200 b. 300 c. 400

4. 650
   a. 600 b. 700 c. 800

5. 472
   a. 300 b. 400 c. 500

6. 547
   a. 500 b. 600 c. 700

A
Round each of these to the nearest 100.

1. 4340
2. 2145
3. 1256
4. 6150
5. 3075
6. 2849
7. 1870
8. 8525
9. 3487

Look at the TU part of the number. If it is 50 or more, round up to the next 100.

B
Round each of these to the nearest 100.

1. 1970
2. 2965
3. 3993
4. 3920
5. 7915
6. 6923
7. 5960
8. 5985
9. 7966

Sometimes when you round to the nearest 100, it pushes the number on into the next 1000.

*So **5960** **rounds up to 6000**.*

C
What must be added to each number to round it up to the next 100?

340   815   562   408

Odds and evens

Warm up Which of these makes an even answer?

1. a 7 + 5   b 3 + 6   c 8 + 5   3. a 10 − 7   b 9 − 5   c 7 − 2
2. a 3 × 3   b 3 × 5   c 2 × 3   4. a 10 ÷ 2   b 12 ÷ 3   c 12 ÷ 4

A Here are some large numbers. Write whether each is an odd or even number.

Odd numbers end in 1, 3, 5, 7 or 9.

1. 236
2. 401
3. 799
4. 994
5. 1356
6. 2765
7. 4278
8. 3009
9. 4770
10. 5231
11. 6632
12. 5124
13. 7843
14. 8667
15. 3574
16. 4687

B Will each answer be 'odd' or 'even'? Write three calculations for each one to prove it.

*You can check some calculations by working out whether answers should be **odd** or **even**.*

1. O + O =
2. E + E =
3. O + E =
4. E + O =
5. O − O =
6. E − E =
7. O − E =
8. E − O =
9. O × O =
10. E × E =
11. O × E =
12. E × O =
13. O ÷ O =
14. E ÷ E =
15. O ÷ E =
16. E ÷ O =

C Choose where to write the missing numbers 2, 3, 4 and 5. Each answer must be even.

14 + ☐   19 − ☐   24 ÷ ☐   5 × ☐

13

Fractions

Warm up

1. How many thirds make one whole?
   a 2   b 3   c 4

2. How many tenths make one whole?
   a 9   b 10   c 100

3. How many quarters make one whole?
   a 2   b 3   c 4

4. How many fifths make one whole?
   a 3   b 4   c 5

5. How many eighths make one whole?
   a 6   b 7   c 8

6. How many sixths make one whole?
   a 4   b 5   c 6

A

Write in the missing numbers.

1. $\frac{1}{2} = \frac{\square}{4}$
2. $\frac{1}{2} = \frac{\square}{10}$
3. $\frac{1}{2} = \frac{\square}{8}$
4. $\frac{1}{2} = \frac{\square}{6}$
5. $\frac{2}{10} = \frac{\square}{5}$
6. $\frac{4}{10} = \frac{\square}{5}$
7. $\frac{6}{10} = \frac{\square}{5}$
8. $\frac{8}{10} = \frac{\square}{5}$

Equivalent fractions look different but are worth the same. Two-quarters are equal to one-half: $\frac{2}{4} = \frac{1}{2}$.

B

What must be added to each of these fractions to make 1?

$\frac{3}{4}$ and $\frac{1}{4}$ are complements of 1. They add up to 1.

1. $\frac{1}{2}$
2. $\frac{4}{5}$
3. $\frac{3}{8}$
4. $\frac{3}{4}$
5. $\frac{2}{5}$
6. $\frac{1}{10}$
7. $\frac{1}{4}$
8. $\frac{1}{8}$
9. $\frac{7}{10}$
10. $\frac{1}{5}$
11. $\frac{5}{8}$
12. $\frac{9}{10}$

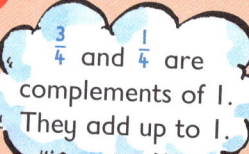

C

Write the three totals.

$\frac{1}{2} + \frac{1}{4}$ $\frac{1}{4} + \frac{1}{4}$ $\frac{3}{4} + \frac{1}{4}$

Rounding measures and money

Warm up Round each number to the nearest 10.

1. 74
 a 60 b 70 c 80

2. 89
 a 70 b 80 c 90

3. 46
 a 30 b 40 c 50

4. 73
 a 70 b 80 c 90

5. 65
 a 50 b 60 c 70

6. 57
 a 40 b 50 c 60

A
Round each of these to the nearest pound.

1. £2.30
2. £6.15
3. £4.84
4. £5.50
5. £7.85
6. £9.08
7. £4.80
8. £2.25
9. £7.48

Look at the pennies part of each amount. If it is 50p or more, you round up to the next pound.

B
Round each of these to the nearest metre, kilogram or litre.

1. 1 m and 60 cm
2. 3 m and 50 cm
3. 7 m and 25 cm
4. 12 m and 90 cm
5. 15 m and 45 cm
6. 19 m and 75 cm
7. 2 kg and 200 g
8. 4 kg and 700 g
9. 1 kg and 500 g
10. 6 kg and 800 g
11. 5 kg and 450 g
12. 8 kg and 550 g
13. 1 ℓ and 500 mℓ
14. 4 ℓ and 600 mℓ
15. 2 ℓ and 100 mℓ
16. 5 ℓ and 900 mℓ
17. 6 ℓ and 250 mℓ
18. 7 ℓ and 750 mℓ

When the measurement is halfway or more between metres, kilograms or litres, you round up.

2 m and 45 cm → 2 m
3 kg and 700 g → 4 kg
7 ℓ and 500 mℓ → 8 ℓ

C
Write each reading to the nearest centimetre.

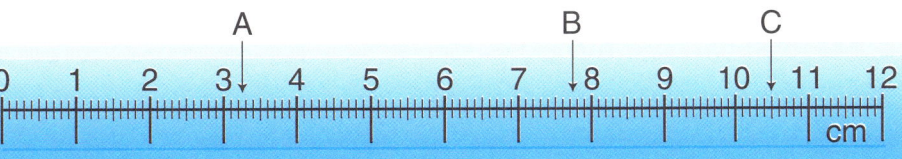

Ordering numbers

Warm up Which is the smallest number in each set?

1 a 563   b 536   c 365   d 635   e 356

2 a 751   b 517   c 175   d 715   e 571

3 a 3075 b 7503 c 5703 d 3057 e 3570

4 a £2.50 b £5.30 c £2.99 d £3.05 e £2.45

5 a £125 b £154 c £109 d £123 e £111

A Write these amounts in order, starting with the smallest.

1 99p   £1.25   80p   £1.50   75p
2 £3.99 219p   £1.09 £1.49   529p
3 £4.25 £3.45   125p   500p   £4.99
4 £0.07 12p   £0.10 £0.02   8p
5 £120   £1.20   102p   £2.01   210p

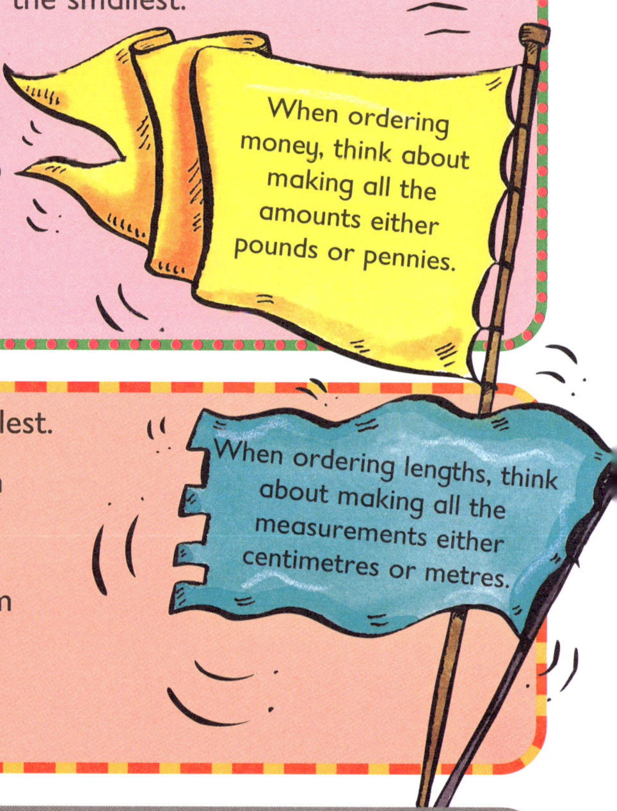

When ordering money, think about making all the amounts either pounds or pennies.

B Write these in order, starting with the smallest.

1 80 cm   1 m   75 cm   1.5 m   95 cm
2 1.30 m   140 cm 99 cm   1.01 m   1.5 m
3 120 cm   1.25 m 129 cm   1.5 m   1.75 m
4 3.5 m   35 cm   3.05 m   53 cm   5.3 m
5 120 m   120 cm 21 m   210 cm   12 m

When ordering lengths, think about making all the measurements either centimetres or metres.

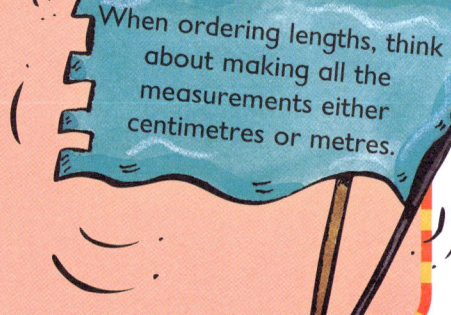

C Write these amounts in order.
Start with the smallest.

£11   £0.75   73p   133p   £1.03

Multiples

Warm up

1. Which number is not part of the 2× table?
   a 16   b 18   c 15   d 12

2. Which number is not part of the 10× table?
   a 40   b 70   c 55   d 100

3. Which number is not part of the 5× table?
   a 45   b 15   c 30   d 32

4. Which number is not part of the 3× table?
   a 9   b 15   c 21   d 25

A

1. What is the twelfth multiple of 2?
2. What is the fifteenth multiple of 5?
3. What is the thirteenth multiple of 10?
4. What is the 20th multiple of 2?
5. What is the 30th multiple of 5?
6. What is the 50th multiple of 10?
7. What is the 100th multiple of 10?
8. What is the sixteenth multiple of 2?
9. What is the seventeenth multiple of 5?
10. What is the nineteenth multiple of 10?
11. What is the 100th multiple of 2?
12. What is the 100th multiple of 5?

Multiples do not end at the tenth one. They go on and on and on…

B

Look for number patterns when finding multiples of large numbers.

Multiples of 5 end in 5 or 0.

Multiples of 25 end in 25, 50, 75 or 00.

Multiples of 2 are always even.

1. Write which of these are multiples of 2.
   120   175   276   378   400   519

2. Write which of these are multiples of 5.
   100   135   250   356   405   558

3. Write which of these are multiples of 25.
   150   375   265   356   760   800

4. Write which of these are multiples of 100.
   700   450   500   900   300   750

C

Which of these numbers are multiples of both 2 and 5?
15   18   30   55   70   52

Which of these numbers are multiples of both 10 and 25?
150   275   175   370   450   500

Halfway

Warm up — Which number is halfway between each of these?

1. 20 and 40   a 25   b 30   c 35
2. 60 and 100   a 70   b 75   c 80
3. 30 and 38   a 32   b 34   c 36

A

Which number is halfway between these?

1. 22 and 34
2. 36 and 48
3. 53 and 69
4. 71 and 87
5. 120 and 130
6. 142 and 154
7. 173 and 185
8. 181 and 199
9. 140 and 180
10. 230 and 270
11. 410 and 450
12. 650 and 690

Drawing a number line can help you to find halfway numbers.

38 ——▲—— 46
     42

B

Which number is halfway between these?

Sometimes the halfway numbers have halves in them. Halfway between 17 and 18 is $17\frac{1}{2}$.

1. 25 and 26
2. 44 and 45
3. 86 and 87
4. 31 and 34
5. 52 and 55
6. 31 and 32
7. 70 and 71
8. 20 and 23
9. 45 and 48
10. 86 and 89

C

Write which number is halfway between these pairs.

67 ——▲—— 72   48 ——▲—— 55   59 ——▲—— 68

Addition and subtraction TU

Warm up
What is the answer to these calculations?

1 20 + 45
    a 55   b 45   c 65

2 24 + 55
    a 75   b 79   c 89

3 126 − 60
    a 66   b 56   c 76

4 73 + 80
    a 143   b 153   c 163

5 87 − 50
    a 27   b 37   c 47

6 88 − 35
    a 53   b 63   c 57

A
Write the answers to these calculations. Write **M** beside answers you can work out in your head.

1 46 + 34
2 39 + 47
3 26 + 68
4 68 + 68
5 27 + 23 + 26
6 27 + 27
7 55 + 28
8 85 + 45
9 75 + 89
10 34 + 19 + 26
11 56 + 77
12 25 + 27 + 45
13 41 + 36 + 19
14 74 + 93
15 29 + 44 + 21
16 25 + 37 + 55

> 34 + 27 + 16
> The order of the adding does not matter. It might be quicker to work out 34 + 16 first.

B
Write the missing digits in the subtractions.

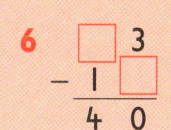

1   5☐
  − 2 8
    2 6

2   5 5
  − 3☐
    1 6

3   ☐1
  − 4☐
    2 6

4   7☐
  − 3 5
    3 7

5   7 0
  − 2☐
    4 3

6   ☐3
  − 1☐
    4 0

> Addition undoes a subtraction. You can check a subtraction by adding.

> Remember always to check your answers.

C
Copy and complete each addition.

   ☐ 4
+ 1 8
   7 ☐

   2 ☐
+ 3 8
   ☐ 5

   ☐ 6
+ 4 ☐
   8 3

Complements

Warm up

1 Which pair total 20?
  a 14, 7
  b 18, 2
  c 16, 3

2 Which pair total 100?
  a 30, 50
  b 20, 60
  c 80, 20

3 Which pair total £1?
  a 20p, 70p
  b 50p, 60p
  c 40p, 60p

4 Which pair total 50p?
  a 15p, 15p
  b 25p, 25p
  c 35p, 35p

5 Which pair total 1 metre?
  a 20 cm, 80 cm
  b 50 cm, 10 cm
  c 90 cm, 20 cm

6 Which pair total 1 kilometre?
  a 300 m, 800 m
  b 500 m, 400 m
  c 900 m, 100 m

A

35 and 65 are **complements** of 100. This means they add up to 100.

600 and 400 are **complements** of 1000. This means they add up to 1000.

What must be added to these to make 1 metre?

1. 55 cm
2. 64 cm
3. 83 cm
4. 19 cm

What must be added to these to make 1 kilogram?

5. 350 g
6. 725 g
7. 710 g
8. 375 g

What must be added to these to make 1 litre?

9. 450 mℓ
10. 850 mℓ
11. 175 mℓ
12. 775 mℓ

B

40 minutes and 20 minutes are **complements** of 1 hour. This means they add up to 1 hour.

What must be added to these to make 1 hour?

1. 50 minutes
2. 20 minutes
3. 15 minutes
4. 25 minutes

What must be added to these to make 1 minute?

5. 30 seconds
6. 10 seconds
7. 35 seconds
8. 25 seconds

What must be added to these to make 1 day?

9. 12 hours
10. 8 hours
11. 4 hours
12. 18 hours

C

What must be added to each of these to make it up to £1?

42p   57p   63p   77p   98p

Calculation words

Warm up

1. Which of these words means **add**?
   a minus
   b plus
   c difference

2. Which of these words means **subtract**?
   a plus
   b total
   c difference

3. Which of these words means **multiply**?
   a minus
   b product
   c plus

A Write the answers.
1. The sum of 27 and 42.
2. 90 minus 46
3. 50 plus 36
4. Increase 43 by 28.
5. Decrease 80 by 64.
6. The difference between 70 and 33.
7. The product of 10 and 20.
8. The total of 35 and 75.
9. The remainder after dividing 28 by 5.
10. The result of halving 70.

Look for the calculation word. Check that your answer seems correct for each problem.

B Answer these word problems.

Read each question carefully. The calculation word does not always tell you what to do.

1. What must I add to 43 to total 75?
2. The sum of two numbers is 78. If one number is 35, what is the other?
3. The difference between two numbers is 15. If the larger number is 50, what is the smaller?
4. The product of two numbers is 24. If one of the numbers is 4, what is the other?
5. Three numbers total 100. If two of the numbers are 34 and 25, what is the third number?

C
Decrease £5 by a half. How much will remain?

Increase £5 by a half. How much will this be altogether?

Money problems 1

Warm up

1. What is the total of these?

   45p   35p

   a 70p
   b 75p
   c 80p

2. What is the change from £1 if you spend:

   65p?

   a 25p
   b 35p
   c 45p

3. What is the total of these?

   25p   55p

   a 70p
   b 80p
   c 90p

4. What is the change from £1 if you spend:

   85p?

   a 5p
   b 15p
   c 25p

A

1. I have three 50p coins and two 20p coins. I spend £1.20. How much will I have left?

2. I have three £1 coins and four 5p coins. I spend £1.80. How much will I have left?

3. I have four £2 coins and five 50p coins. I spend £9.40. How much will I have left?

4. I have two £2 coins and six 20p coins. I spend £4.90. How much will I have left?

Sometimes you have to work out a problem in more than one step.

B

1. I bought three books costing 90p, 75p and £1.99. What was my change from £5?

2. I received 65p change from £10. How much did I spend?

3. I bought two toys costing 80p and £1.75. My change was £2.45. What money did I pay with?

4. What is the total of 85p, £2.70 and £5?

5. How much change will I get from £10 if I buy two magazines costing £3.99 each?

Be careful when some information is in pennies and some is in pounds. Decide which to work in and make them all the same.

C

Will has £2.30 but Tanya has twice as much.

How much do they have in total?

Measurement problems 1

Warm up

1. How many centimetres are there in half a metre?
   a 50
   b 500
   c 5000

2. How many millilitres are there in half a litre?
   a 50
   b 500
   c 5000

3. How many grams are there in half a kilogram?
   a 50
   b 500
   c 5000

4. How many seconds are there in half a minute?
   a 30
   b 50
   c 60

A

1. What is the difference in length between 1 m and 45 cm?
2. What is the total of 400 g, 350 g and 120 g?
3. Increase half a litre by 200 ml.
4. Decrease half a kilogram by 150 g.
5. Add one and a half metres to 40 cm.

There are 100 cm in 1 m, 1000 g in 1 kg and 1000 ml in 1 l.

B

1. I went to bed at 8:45pm and read for 25 minutes. When did I stop reading?
2. I put a cake in the oven at 10:50am and took it out at 11:25am. How long was it in the oven?
3. I started work at 11:45am and finished at 12:35pm. How long was I working?
4. I started eating at 4:25pm and finished 50 minutes later. When did I finish eating?
5. I went playing at noon and returned one and a half hours later. At what time did I return?

We write time like this – 3:45. This means 45 minutes past 3 o'clock.
1 hour = 60 minutes

C

How much further is one and a half kilometres than one and a quarter kilometres? Write your answer in metres.

Multiplication tables

Warm up Which multiplication fact matches these answers?

1. 16
   a 3 × 5
   b 4 × 4
   c 2 × 9

2. 20
   a 4 × 6
   b 2 × 9
   c 5 × 4

3. 12
   a 6 × 2
   b 3 × 3
   c 2 × 4

4. 30
   a 2 × 10
   b 6 × 5
   c 5 × 7

5. 21
   a 4 × 5
   b 10 × 2
   c 3 × 7

6. 15
   a 3 × 4
   b 3 × 6
   c 5 × 3

A Work these out.

1. 5 × 5
   5 × 50

2. 2 × 9
   2 × 90

3. 10 × 7
   10 × 70

4. 6 × 2
   60 × 2

5. 7 × 5
   70 × 5

6. 8 × 10
   80 × 10

7. 4 × 4
   4 × 40

8. 3 × 4
   30 × 4

9. 6 × 4
   6 × 40

You can use your table facts to work out other facts.
5 × 4 = 20
5 × 40 = 200

B Now try these.

1. 2 × 9
   4 × 9

2. 2 × 6
   4 × 6

3. 2 × 7
   4 × 7

4. 3 × 4
   6 × 4

5. 3 × 6
   6 × 6

6. 3 × 7
   6 × 7

7. 3 × 9
   6 × 9

8. 3 × 3
   6 × 3

9. 3 × 8
   6 × 8

10. 4 × 3
    8 × 3

11. 4 × 5
    8 × 5

12. 4 × 4
    8 × 4

Doubling tables you know can be useful:
- doubling the 2× table gives the 4× table
- doubling the 3× table gives the 6× table
- doubling the 4× table gives the 8× table

C Look at the number machine. Copy and complete the table.

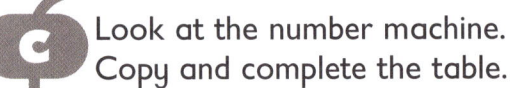

In	7		4	
Out		27	18	3

Doubling

Warm up
What is double each of these?

1. 15   a 20   b 30   c 40
2. 17   a 34   b 35   c 36
3. 35   a 50   b 60   c 70
4. 14   a 26   b 28   c 32
5. 45   a 80   b 90   c 100
6. 18   a 26   b 36   c 46

A
Double each of these.

1. 21
2. 24
3. 26
4. 28
5. 29
6. 34
7. 42
8. 51
9. 63
10. 74
11. 38
12. 46
13. 59
14. 77
15. 96
16. 120
17. 140
18. 160
19. 170
20. 190

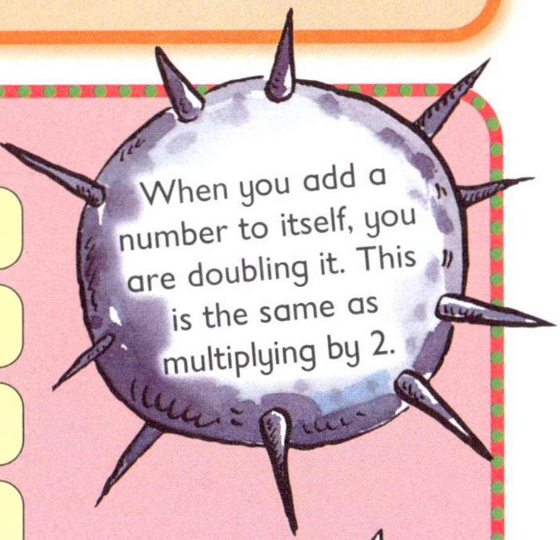

When you add a number to itself, you are doubling it. This is the same as multiplying by 2.

B
Which measurement is twice these?

1. 35 cm
2. 28 cm
3. 74 cm
4. 97 cm
5. 86 cm
6. 240 ml
7. 320 ml
8. 410 ml
9. 630 ml
10. 750 ml
11. 190 g
12. 370 g
13. 580 g
14. 660 g
15. 760 g

Twice a number is the same as doubling. Twice 310 ml is 620 ml.

C
Look at the number machine.
Copy and complete the table.

In					
Out	84	182	268	500	850

Mental problems

Warm up Which answers are the same?

1. $7 + 8$ — a $9 + 4$ b $8 + 6$ c $5 + 10$
2. $9 + 5$ — a $20 - 4$ b 7×2 c $8 + 4$
3. $19 - 6$ — a $20 - 6$ b $15 - 2$ c $17 - 3$
4. $20 - 4$ — a $18 - 4$ b $8 + 6$ c 4×4
5. 2×9 — a 4×4 b 5×3 c 3×6
6. 3×4 — a $20 - 8$ b $9 + 4$ c 2×7

A

Work out the answers in your head. Jot each answer down if it helps to solve the problems.

Answer the word problems.

1. What must be subtracted from 7×10 to equal $50 + 4$?
2. What must be subtracted from 7×5 to equal $40 - 25$?
3. What must be subtracted from $25 + 35$ to equal 10×5?
4. What must be subtracted from $18 + 16$ to equal 6×5?
5. What must be subtracted from $60 - 35$ to equal 2×9?

B

Answer the word problems.

1. What must be added to $30 - 18$ to equal 8×3?
2. What must be added to 2×7 to equal $50 - 35$?
3. What must be added to $24 + 36$ to equal 10×10?
4. What must be added to $80 - 64$ to equal 5×8?
5. What must be added to 3×5 to equal 10×7?

Try to do these in your head. Always look at your answer to see if it seems sensible.

C

Each side must have the same answer so that they balance.

What is the missing number?

$100 - 76 \quad\quad 4 \times \square$

Missing digits

Warm up
What is the missing number?

1. $8 + \square = 40$ a 22   b 32   c 42
2. $27 + \square = 100$ a 63   b 73   c 83
3. $5 \times \square = 100$ a 20   b 25   c 30
4. $2 \times \square = 86$ a 33   b 43   c 53
5. $100 - \square = 37$ a 53   b 73   c 63
6. $70 - \square = 14$ a 56   b 46   c 66

A
What are the missing digits?

1. $3\square + \square 2 = 117$
2. $4\square + \square 6 = 128$
3. $6\square + \square 5 = 136$
4. $5\square + \square 8 = 109$
5. $5\square - \square 2 = 24$
6. $6\square - \square 5 = 12$
7. $4\square - \square 1 = 26$
8. $9\square - \square 3 = 53$

There are only ten digits: 0, 1, 2, 3, 4, 5, 6, 7, 8 and 9.

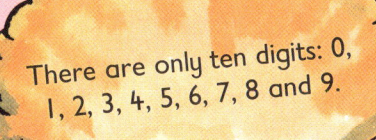

B
What are the missing digits?

1. $2\square + \square 7 = 92$
2. $4\square + \square 6 = 70$
3. $6\square + \square 4 = 93$
4. $5\square + \square 8 = 84$
5. $5\square + \square 2 = 111$
6. $6\square + \square 8 = 102$
7. $9\square + \square 7 = 125$
8. $8\square + \square 6 = 142$

Think about what happens when the tens or units total 10 or more.

38 + 27

86 + 57

C
Work out the missing digits.

Mental differences

Warm up
What is the answer?

1) 124 − 80   a 40 b 44 c 46
2) 100 − 64   a 44 b 36 c 46
3) 137 − 90   a 27 b 37 c 47
4) 100 − 17   a 93 b 83 c 87
5) 142 − 60   a 72 b 82 c 88
6) 100 − 58   a 48 b 42 c 52

A
Write down the difference between these numbers. Work it out in your head.

1) 5   160
2) 7   310
3) 4   580
4) 3   770
5) 250 8
6) 370 4
7) 430 6
8) 920 7
9) 152 6
10) 473 8
11) 5   212
12) 4   351

The difference is how many more or less one number is than another. You can find the difference by subtracting the smaller number from the larger. The difference between 200 and 6 is 194.

B
When two numbers are close, you can find the difference by counting on from one to the other. The difference between 348 and 352 is 4.

Write down the differences between these close numbers.

1) 188 193
2) 218 221
3) 365 356
4) 671 667
5) 999 1003
6) 996 1006
7) 1005 997
8) 1008 998

C
Work out the missing numbers.

405 − ☐ = 397   996 + ☐ = 1005

Adding nines

Warm up
What is the answer?

1. 137 + 10
   - a 138
   - b 147
   - c 237

2. 1267 + 100
   - a 1277
   - b 1367
   - c 1377

3. 476 + 10
   - a 486
   - b 487
   - c 576

4. 2067 + 100
   - a 2167
   - b 2077
   - c 3067

5. 598 + 10
   - a 698
   - b 608
   - c 618

6. 3977 + 100
   - a 4087
   - b 3987
   - c 4077

A
Add 9 to each of these numbers.

1. 46
2. 57
3. 72
4. 88
5. 95
6. 126
7. 254
8. 406
9. 559
10. 835
11. 298
12. 396
13. 792
14. 896
15. 996
16. 1256
17. 1689
18. 2405
19. 3372
20. 2637

A quick way to add 9 is to add on 10 then subtract 1. Try to do this in your head.

B
Add 99 to each of these numbers.

A quick way to add 99 is to add on 100 then subtract 1. Try to do this in your head.

1. 256
2. 372
3. 407
4. 688
5. 798
6. 1428
7. 3642
8. 7684
9. 6834
10. 5566
11. 1935
12. 2940
13. 5946
14. 6902
15. 3999

C
Look at the number machine.
Copy and complete the table.

In					
Out	64	162	751	500	903

Adding 2-digit numbers

Warm up

What is the answer?

1. 132 + 16
   - a 292
   - b 148
   - c 146

2. 128 + 61
   - a 189
   - b 738
   - c 188

3. 411 + 24
   - a 435
   - b 651
   - c 415

4. 330 + 44
   - a 770
   - b 370
   - c 374

5. 305 + 31
   - a 335
   - b 615
   - c 336

6. 223 + 65
   - a 288
   - b 873
   - c 285

A

Try to work these out in your head.

1. 148 + 39
2. 165 + 49
3. 186 + 29
4. 256 + 59
5. 376 + 49
6. 425 + 49
7. 254 + 89
8. 406 + 79
9. 559 + 69
10. 335 + 29
11. 246 + 49
12. 447 + 89
13. 872 + 69
14. 337 + 59
15. 265 + 79

There is a quick way to add on numbers ending in 9. Add on the next number, then subtract 1.
127 + 39 = 127 + 40 − 1

B

Write the answers to these calculations.
Write **M** beside answers you can work out in your head.

1. 124 + 43
2. 232 + 57
3. 314 + 43
4. 522 + 66
5. 705 + 54
6. 245 + 38
7. 146 + 47
8. 318 + 55
9. 745 + 36
10. 837 + 47
11. 253 + 62
12. 197 + 72
13. 465 + 84
14. 365 + 85
15. 467 + 88

One way is to add on the tens digit first, then the units.
256 + 43
256 + 40 = 296
296 + 3 = 299

C

Work out the missing digits.

```
  7 3 ☐         2 ☐ ☐         2 5 6
+   ☐ 6       +   3 3       + ☐ ☐
─────────     ─────────     ─────────
  7 7 0         2 8 1         3 3 2
```

Subtracting nines

Warm up — What is the answer?

1. 284 − 10
   - a 184
   - b 274
   - c 294

2. 1267 − 100
   - a 1257
   - b 1167
   - c 1157

3. 506 − 10
   - a 496
   - b 516
   - c 495

4. 2417 − 100
   - a 2317
   - b 2407
   - c 1417

5. 818 − 10
   - a 198
   - b 808
   - c 817

6. 2456 − 100
   - a 2366
   - b 2346
   - c 2356

A

Subtract 9 from each of these numbers.

1. 38
2. 44
3. 65
4. 88
5. 94
6. 147
7. 338
8. 728
9. 792
10. 917
11. 406
12. 501
13. 608
14. 703
15. 807
16. 1327
17. 1168
18. 1057
19. 2305
20. 4169

A quick way to subtract 9 is to subtract 10, then add 1. Try to do this in your head.

B

A quick way to subtract 99 is to subtract 100, then add 1. Try to do this in your head.

Subtract 99 from each of these numbers.

1. 295
2. 403
3. 485
4. 725
5. 816
6. 1185
7. 2192
8. 3666
9. 4286
10. 6382
11. 2074
12. 2089
13. 3061
14. 5075
15. 6003

C

Look at the number machine. Copy and complete the table.

In					
Out	72	116	353	506	721

Subtracting 2-digit numbers

Warm up
What is the answer?

1. 186 – 15
   - a 135
   - b 56
   - c 171

2. 477 – 25
   - a 452
   - b 425
   - c 227

3. 357 – 24
   - a 333
   - b 117
   - c 315

4. 836 – 32
   - a 516
   - b 813
   - c 804

5. 285 – 24
   - a 243
   - b 261
   - c 45

6. 786 – 62
   - a 760
   - b 166
   - c 724

A
Try to do these in your head.

1. 165 – 39
2. 264 – 49
3. 296 – 29
4. 582 – 59
5. 663 – 49
6. 248 – 49
7. 386 – 89
8. 472 – 79
9. 417 – 69
10. 603 – 29
11. 419 – 49
12. 319 – 29
13. 519 – 69
14. 339 – 59
15. 269 – 79

There is a quick way to subtract numbers ending in 9. Subtract the next number, then add on 1.
127 – 39 =
127 – 40 + 1

B
Work out the answers to these calculations.
Write **M** beside any answers you can work out in your head.

One way to work these out is to subtract the tens digit first, then the units.
212 – 43
212 – 40 = 172
172 – 3 = 169

1. 253 – 42
2. 375 – 54
3. 282 – 43
4. 442 – 27
5. 581 – 54
6. 245 – 62
7. 316 – 44
8. 407 – 55
9. 518 – 36
10. 837 – 42
11. 253 – 68
12. 304 – 75
13. 465 – 87
14. 365 – 88
15. 403 – 66

C
Copy and put in the missing digits.

```
  4 3 □
 –  □ 6
  ─────
  4 0 4
```

```
  2 1 6
 –  □ □
  ─────
  1 8 7
```

```
  4 □ 6
 –  7 □
  ─────
  3 3 6
```

Addition HTU

Warm up
What is the answer to these calculations?

1. 245 + 40
   - a 649
   - b 249
   - c 285

2. 385 + 500
   - a 885
   - b 855
   - c 435

3. 375 + 20
   - a 377
   - b 575
   - c 395

4. 125 + 800
   - a 185
   - b 925
   - c 305

5. 327 + 80
   - a 407
   - b 307
   - c 387

6. 300 + 505
   - a 805
   - b 535
   - c 835

A

Answer these calculations.

The order of addition does not matter. 129 + 456 is the same as 456 + 129.

1. 345 + 26
2. 447 + 74
3. 826 + 86
4. 754 + 66
5. 204 + 136
6. 295 + 395
7. 318 + 548
8. 365 + 475
9. 566 + 748
10. 765 + 893
11. 849 + 499
12. 875 + 287

B

Now try these.

Estimate each total before working it out. 176 + 482 + 208 is about 200 + 500 + 200 = 900

1. 286 + 167 + 887
2. 548 + 995 + 718
3. 347 + 608 + 389
4. 442 + 581 + 46
5. 79 + 137 + 463
6. 795 + 88 + 385
7. 175 + 87 + 56
8. 846 + 374 + 39

C

Copy and complete each addition.

```
  2 3 □
+ 3 □ 5
-------
  5 7 8
```

```
  3 7 □
+ 3 □ 6
-------
  6 9 2
```

```
  2 6 □
+ 4 □ 8
-------
  7 0 1
```

Subtraction HTU

Warm up — What is the answer to these calculations?

1. 345 − 40
   - a 295
   - b 385
   - c 305

2. 385 − 200
   - a 365
   - b 585
   - c 185

3. 465 − 20
   - a 265
   - b 445
   - c 485

4. 725 − 500
   - a 225
   - b 720
   - c 675

5. 320 − 80
   - a 240
   - b 400
   - c 312

6. 649 − 400
   - a 249
   - b 609
   - c 645

A What is the missing number?

1. 345 − 26 = ☐
2. 447 − 28 = ☐
3. 826 − 47 = ☐
4. 754 − 56 = ☐
5. 204 − ☐ = 194
6. 295 − ☐ = 180
7. 437 − ☐ = 218
8. 815 − ☐ = 537
9. ☐ − 77 = 237
10. ☐ − 76 = 345
11. ☐ − 48 = 264
12. ☐ − 35 = 601

You can check a subtraction by addition.
374 − 88 = 286
check
286 + 88 = 374

B Write one checking addition for each subtraction.

One checking addition for 345 − 176 is 169 + 176 because 345 − 176 = 169.

1. 672 − 238
2. 405 − 285
3. 655 − 195
4. 845 − 385
5. 667 − 299
6. 867 − 654
7. 604 − 278
8. 505 − 268

C Copy and complete each subtraction.

```
  3 6 ☐        4 0 ☐        7 3 ☐
− 1 ☐ 8      − 1 ☐ 5      − 4 ☐ 6
  2 3 1        2 6 2        3 0 8
```

34

Division 1

Warm up
What is the answer to these calculations?

1. 18 ÷ 2   a 7   b 8   c 9
2. 24 ÷ 4   a 6   b 7   c 8
3. 12 ÷ 3   a 3   b 4   c 5
4. 20 ÷ 2   a 8   b 9   c 10
5. 35 ÷ 5   a 6   b 7   c 8
6. 45 ÷ 5   a 7   b 8   c 9

A
Write the missing numbers.

1. 26 ÷ 2 = ☐
2. 36 ÷ 3 = ☐
3. 44 ÷ 4 = ☐
4. 60 ÷ 5 = ☐
5. 28 ÷ ☐ = 14
6. 70 ÷ ☐ = 14
7. 84 ÷ ☐ = 21
8. 69 ÷ ☐ = 23
9. ☐ ÷ 3 = 13
10. ☐ ÷ 5 = 15
11. ☐ ÷ 2 = 25
12. ☐ ÷ 4 = 22

You can check a division by multiplication.
24 ÷ 2 = 12
check 12 × 2 = 24

B
Answer these in your head.

1. 30 ÷ 2 = ☐
2. 90 ÷ 3 = ☐
3. 80 ÷ 4 = ☐
4. 70 ÷ 5 = ☐
5. 50 ÷ 2 = ☐
6. 70 ÷ 2 = ☐
7. 60 ÷ 3 = ☐
8. 90 ÷ 5 = ☐
9. 80 ÷ 5 = ☐
10. 90 ÷ 2 = ☐
11. 500 ÷ 2 = ☐
12. 600 ÷ 3 = ☐
13. 800 ÷ 4 = ☐
14. 600 ÷ 5 = ☐
15. 300 ÷ 2 = ☐

To divide by 4, you can divide by 2 and then 2 again.
60 ÷ 4 = 60 ÷ 2 ÷ 2 =
60 ÷ 2 = 30 and
30 ÷ 2 = 15

C
Work out the missing numbers.

30 ÷ ☐ = 15   60 ÷ ☐ = 15

☐ ÷ 3 = 15   ☐ ÷ 5 = 15

Division 2

Warm up

Work these out.

1. 30 ÷ 2
   - a 14
   - b 15
   - c 16

2. 80 ÷ 4
   - a 18
   - b 20
   - c 22

3. 90 ÷ 3
   - a 30
   - b 40
   - c 50

4. 70 ÷ 2
   - a 30
   - b 35
   - c 40

5. 60 ÷ 5
   - a 12
   - b 14
   - c 16

6. 70 ÷ 5
   - a 12
   - b 13
   - c 14

A

Try to answer some of these in your head.

To divide 2-digit numbers, divide the tens number first and then the units.

86 ÷ 2

80 ÷ 2 = 40 and 6 ÷ 2 = 3

So the answer is 43.

1. 42 ÷ 2 =
2. 63 ÷ 3 =
3. 88 ÷ 4 =
4. 64 ÷ 2 =
5. 69 ÷ 3 =
6. 34 ÷ 2 =
7. 96 ÷ 3 =
8. 48 ÷ 4 =
9. 56 ÷ 2 =
10. 78 ÷ 2 =
11. 55 ÷ 5 =
12. 95 ÷ 5 =
13. 65 ÷ 5 =
14. 85 ÷ 5 =
15. 75 ÷ 5 =

B

Write the missing numbers.

To divide by 4, you can divide by 2 and then 2 again.

60 ÷ 4 =
60 ÷ 2 ÷ 2 =
60 ÷ 2 = 30 and 30 ÷ 2 = 15

1. 48 ÷ 4 =
2. 84 ÷ 4 =
3. 64 ÷ 4 =
4. 72 ÷ 4 =
5. 52 ÷ 4 =
6. 56 ÷ 4 =
7. 68 ÷ 4 =
8. 76 ÷ 4 =
9. 96 ÷ 4 =
10. 92 ÷ 4 =
11. 120 ÷ 4 =
12. 200 ÷ 4 =
13. 160 ÷ 4 =
14. 140 ÷ 4 =
15. 180 ÷ 4 =

C

Share £1.20 between Jack, Chloe and Jay.

How much will each receive?

Remainders 1

Warm up
What is the remainder?

1. $26 \div 3$ — a 0 b 1 c 2
2. $67 \div 10$ — a 6 b 7 c 8
3. $34 \div 5$ — a 2 b 3 c 4
4. $47 \div 5$ — a 2 b 3 c 4
5. $34 \div 4$ — a 1 b 2 c 3
6. $32 \div 3$ — a 1 b 2 c 3

A
Write the answer and the remainder.

1. $25 \div 2 =$ ☐
2. $31 \div 2 =$ ☐
3. $57 \div 2 =$ ☐
4. $69 \div 2 =$ ☐
5. $32 \div 5 =$ ☐
6. $54 \div 5 =$ ☐
7. $68 \div 5 =$ ☐
8. $81 \div 5 =$ ☐
9. $17 \div 3 =$ ☐
10. $23 \div 3 =$ ☐
11. $31 \div 3 =$ ☐
12. $64 \div 3 =$ ☐

Remainders are sometimes written like this:
$40 \div 3 = 13$ r1

B
Work out the number that is being divided.

1. Divide by 2. The result is 11 r1.
2. Divide by 5. The result is 6 r3.
3. Divide by 10. The result is 7 r8.
4. Divide by 3. The result is 8 r1.
5. Divide by 4. The result is 5 r3.
6. Divide by 5. The result is 12 r2.

Multiplication undoes division.
$24 \div 3 = 8$, check $8 \times 3 = 24$
$22 \div 5 = 4$ r2, check $4 \times 5 = 20$ plus the remaining $2 = 22$.

C
What are the missing numbers?

$19 \div$ ☐ $= 6$ r1 $29 \div$ ☐ $= 5$ r4 $39 \div$ ☐ $= 4$ r3

Remainders 2

Warm up
What is the remainder?

1. 238 ÷ 10
   - a 2
   - b 8
   - c 3

2. 567 ÷ 10
   - a 6
   - b 7
   - c 5

3. 485 ÷ 10
   - a 5
   - b 4
   - c 8

4. 632 ÷ 10
   - a 2
   - b 6
   - c 3

5. 319 ÷ 10
   - a 1
   - b 3
   - c 9

6. 954 ÷ 10
   - a 5
   - b 4
   - c 9

A
Write the answers.

1. Share 17p between 2 children. How much will child receive?
2. Divide 34 marbles between 4 children. How many marbles will each child get?
3. Share 29 CDs amongst 5 children. How many CDs will each child have?
4. Arrange 26 spoons into 3 equal sets. How many spoons are there in each set?
5. Put 43 people into two teams. How many people are in each team?
6. Divide £1.25 between 2 children. How much will each get?

Sometimes you have to ignore the remainder.

B
Write the answers.

1. 4 children can sit round a table. How many tables are needed for 19 children?
2. 10 buns fit in each baking tray. How many trays are needed for 64 buns?
3. 5 people can travel in a car. How many cars are needed for 13 people?
4. Pencils are sold in packs of 4. How many packs do I need to have 32 pencils?
5. 10 stickers are placed on a page. How many pages are needed for 126 stickers?
6. Tins of juice are sold in packs of 3. How many packs are needed for 32 tins?

Sometimes you have to look at the remainder and round up.

C
A bus holds 45 people. How many buses will be needed for 120 people?

Halving

Warm up
What is a half of these?

1. 46 — a 22 b 23 c 24
2. 30 — a 15 b 16 c 17
3. 84 — a 42 b 43 c 44
4. 50 — a 15 b 25 c 35
5. 62 — a 30 b 31 c 32
6. 90 — a 35 b 45 c 55

A
What is half of each number?

1. 18
2. 15
3. 19
4. 11
5. 13
6. 20
7. 27
8. 23
9. 25
10. 29
11. 60
12. 63
13. 67
14. 66
15. 61
16. 30
17. 33
18. 36
19. 35
20. 39

Sometimes when you halve a number, there is a half in the answer. Half of 17 is $8\frac{1}{2}$.

B
You can write halves in several ways.
$\frac{1}{2}$ of 3 metres is $1\frac{1}{2}$ metres.
or 1 metre and 50 centimetres
or 1.50 m.

Write each answer in two ways.

1. Half of 7 metres
2. Half of 11 metres
3. Half of 15 metres
4. Half of 23 metres
5. Half of 31 metres
6. Half of 5 litres
7. Half of 9 litres
8. Half of 13 litres
9. Half of 3 kilograms
10. Half of 17 kilograms

C
How many minutes are there in half of 3 hours?

Money problems 2

Warm up
What is the answer?

1. The total of 3 books costing £5 each.
   - a £15
   - b £16
   - c £17

2. If 2 books cost £1.20, what will 1 book cost?
   - a £1.00
   - b 80p
   - c 60p

3. The total of 5 toys costing 40p each.
   - a 200p
   - b 240p
   - c 160p

4. If 4 toys cost £12, what will 1 toy cost?
   - a £2
   - b £3
   - c £4

5. The total of 4 comics costing 20p each.
   - a 70p
   - b 80p
   - c 90p

6. If 5 comics cost 65p, what will 1 comic cost?
   - a 12p
   - b 13p
   - c 14p

A
1. I buy five books costing £3 each. How much change from £20?
2. I buy four tickets costing £7 each. How many £10 notes will I need to pay for them?
3. I buy three £6 toys and two £8 toys. What is the total cost?
4. I buy two cakes and my change from £5 is £2. How much does each cake cost?
5. I buy three tickets for a total of £6. What would two tickets cost?
6. 10 stickers cost £7. What will 1 sticker cost?

Sometimes you have to work out part of the problem before reaching the answer.

B

Sometimes it is easier to change pounds into pence to work calculations out.

1. Jules saves 25p each week. How many weeks before he has saved £5.50?
2. Jenny bought three packets at £1.20 each. What was her change from £5?
3. Share £2.40 between Rolf, Wendy, Jo and Parveen. How much will they have each?
4. Dad shares £5 between his 4 children. How much will they each receive?
5. Reese saves £1.30 each week. How much will she have saved in 5 weeks?

C
Lee, Frances and Tom want to buy both presents and they each want to pay the same amount. If the presents cost £1.30 and £2.60, how much will they each pay?

£1.30

£2.60

Measurement problems 2

Warm up

What is the answer?

1. How many millilitres are in 1 litre?
   a 10
   b 100
   c 1000

2. How many millilitres are in half a litre?
   a 500
   b 50
   c 5000

3. How many centimetres are in 1 metre?
   a 10
   b 100
   c 1000

4. How many centimetres are in half a metre?
   a 50
   b 5
   c 500

5. How many grams are in 1 kg?
   a 100
   b 1000
   c 10

7. How many grams are in half a kilogram?
   a 5
   b 50
   c 500

A

1. A teaspoon holds 5 ml. How many spoonsful are there in half a litre?
2. How many 25 cm lengths of string can be cut from half a metre?
3. How many 100 g weights will balance half a kilogram?
4. A litre bottle has 250 ml and 450 ml poured out. How much remains in the bottle?
5. One egg weighs about 50 g. What will the weight of 6 eggs be?
6. Two lengths of ribbon measure 80 cm and $1\frac{1}{2}$ m. What is the difference between them?

You need to know how many:
centimetres are in 1 m,
millilitres are in 1 l,
grams are in 1 kg.

B

1. Total 60 cm, $\frac{1}{2}$ m and $1\frac{1}{2}$ m.
2. Total 200 g, $\frac{1}{2}$ kg and $1\frac{1}{2}$ kg.
3. Total 25 ml, $\frac{1}{2}$ litre and 1 litre.
4. Total 75 cm, $\frac{1}{2}$ m and $\frac{1}{4}$ m.
5. Subtract 300 g from $1\frac{1}{2}$ kg.
6. Subtract 700 ml from $1\frac{1}{2}$ litres.
7. Subtract 250 ml from $\frac{1}{2}$ litre.
8. Subtract 150 g from $\frac{1}{4}$ kg.

Look carefully at the units. You might need to change: metres to centimetres, kilograms to grams, litres to millilitres.

C

A large potato weighs about $\frac{1}{4}$ kg. How many large potatoes will weigh 3 kg? What will 20 large potatoes weigh?

Tens and hundreds

Warm up

What is the answer?

1. 30 × 10
   - a 300
   - b 3000
   - c 30

2. 500 ÷ 10
   - a 5
   - b 50
   - c 500

3. 50 × 10
   - a 500
   - b 50
   - c 5000

4. 200 ÷ 10
   - a 20
   - b 2
   - c 200

5. 70 × 10
   - a 70
   - b 700
   - c 7000

6. 300 ÷ 10
   - a 3
   - b 30
   - c 300

A

Multiply each number by 10.

1. 30
2. 50
3. 25
4. 65
5. 95
6. 400
7. 200
8. 600
9. 250
10. 750

Multiply each number by 100.

11. 4
12. 7
13. 8
14. 10
15. 12
16. 20
17. 40
18. 50
19. 80
20. 90

Think carefully about what happens to the digits when you multiply by 10 and 100.

B

Think carefully about what happens to the digits when you divide by 10 and 100.

Divide each number by 10.

1. 200
2. 500
3. 350
4. 550
5. 870
6. 3000
7. 8000
8. 6500
9. 2500
10. 8500

Divide each number by 100.

11. 300
12. 600
13. 800
14. 2000
15. 7000
16. 1500
17. 3500
18. 4500
19. 5600
20. 7200

C

Work out the missing numbers.

100 × ☐ = 1000
100 ÷ ☐ = 1

100 × ☐ = 100
100 ÷ ☐ = 10

Multiplication TU

Warm up
What is the answer?

1. 30 × 3
   - a 60
   - b 90
   - c 900

2. 20 × 5
   - a 100
   - b 1000
   - c 500

3. 50 × 4
   - a 20
   - b 2000
   - c 200

4. 60 × 3
   - a 18
   - b 1800
   - c 180

5. 70 × 2
   - a 14
   - b 140
   - c 702

6. 20 × 7
   - a 14
   - b 140
   - c 207

A
Work out the answers to these.

1. 11 × 5
2. 32 × 3
3. 42 × 2
4. 12 × 4
5. 27 × 2
6. 18 × 4
7. 19 × 5
8. 26 × 3
9. 36 × 2
10. 15 × 5
11. 24 × 3
12. 19 × 4

26 × 2
2 twenties are 40 and 2 sixes are 12, so the answer is 52

B
Answer these.

1. 53 × 2
2. 42 × 3
3. 31 × 5
4. 32 × 4
5. 61 × 2
6. 52 × 4
7. 65 × 5
8. 55 × 3
9. 56 × 2
10. 45 × 5
11. 34 × 3
12. 53 × 4

Sometimes the answer will be more than 100.
46 × 3
3 forties are 120 and 3 sixes are 18, so the answer is 138.

C
What are the missing numbers?

14 × ☐ = 70
23 × ☐ = 69

45 × ☐ = 180
53 × ☐ = 159

Calculation links

Warm up
What are the missing numbers?

1. $24 \div \square = 6$
   - a 3
   - b 4
   - c 2

2. $24 + \square = 70$
   - a 44
   - b 46
   - c 94

3. $4 \times \square = 80$
   - a 20
   - b 40
   - c 30

4. $\square - 15 = 60$
   - a 45
   - b 75
   - c 55

5. $\square \div 3 = 21$
   - a 63
   - b 7
   - c 24

6. $\square + 25 = 80$
   - a 105
   - b 45
   - c 55

A
Answer each of these.
Then write three more add and subtract facts for each calculation.

1. $72 + 12$
2. $53 + 22$
3. $18 + 27$
4. $25 + 28$
5. $80 - 35$
6. $50 - 17$
7. $48 - 26$
8. $51 - 19$
9. $55 + 85$
10. $78 + 44$
11. $120 - 40$
12. $150 - 15$

$14 + 36 = 50$
Using this fact, you also know:
$36 + 14 = 50$
$50 - 14 = 36$
$50 - 36 = 14$
These are linked add and subtract facts.

B
Answer each of these.
Then write three more add and subtract facts for each calculation.

1. 13×3
2. 42×2
3. 21×4
4. 13×5
5. $30 \div 2$
6. $39 \div 3$
7. $84 \div 4$
8. $55 \div 5$
9. 46×2
10. 57×3
11. $120 \div 2$
12. $150 \div 5$

$23 \times 3 = 69$
Using this fact, you also know:
$3 \times 23 = 69$
$69 \div 23 = 3$
$69 \div 3 = 23$
These are linked multiply and divide facts.

C
If $246 + 368 = 614$, what is $614 - 246$?

If $128 \div 4 = 32$, what is $128 \div 32$?

Triples

Warm up
What are the answers?

1) $4 + 7 + 9$
  - a 19
  - b 20
  - c 21

2) $20 + 15 + 25$
  - a 50
  - b 60
  - c 70

3) $12 + 5 - 6$
  - a 9
  - b 10
  - c 11

4) $50 - 35 + 5$
  - a 20
  - b 15
  - c 25

5) $19 - 12 + 6$
  - a 13
  - b 14
  - c 15

6) $75 - 30 + 15$
  - a 60
  - b 65
  - c 55

A
Write the answers.

1) $3 \times 4 \times 2$
2) $2 \times 4 \times 5$
3) $3 \times 3 \times 2$
4) $5 \times 2 \times 2$
5) $2 \times 2 \times 2$
6) $4 \times 4 \times 5$
7) $3 \times 4 \times 3$
8) $3 \times 3 \times 3$
9) $4 \times 5 \times 3$
10) $5 \times 5 \times 4$
11) $4 \times 4 \times 4$
12) $5 \times 4 \times 2$
13) $3 \times 3 \times 2$
14) $2 \times 3 \times 4$
15) $5 \times 5 \times 5$
16) $5 \times 4 \times 3$

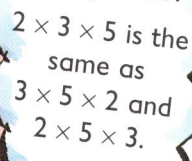

You can multiply in any order. $2 \times 3 \times 5$ is the same as $3 \times 5 \times 2$ and $2 \times 5 \times 3$.

B
Write the answers.

Work out the answer in the brackets first. $5 \times (10 - 4) = 5 \times 6 = 30$.

1) $4 \times (12 - 8)$
2) $12 \div (8 - 6)$
3) $5 \times (4 + 4)$
4) $20 \div (7 + 3)$
5) $(4 + 3) \times 3$
6) $(10 - 5) \times 4$
7) $(8 + 4) \div 2$
8) $(18 - 3) \div 5$
9) $(2 \times 3) + 7$
10) $(5 \times 5) - 6$
11) $(20 \div 4) + 8$
12) $(50 \div 5) - 3$

C
What are the missing signs?

$4 \,\square\, 6 \,\square\, 2 = 8$

$8 \,\square\, 4 \,\square\, 2 = 30$

$6 \,\square\, 3 \,\square\, 4 = 12$

$+$ $\times$ $-$ $\div$

Shape knowledge 1

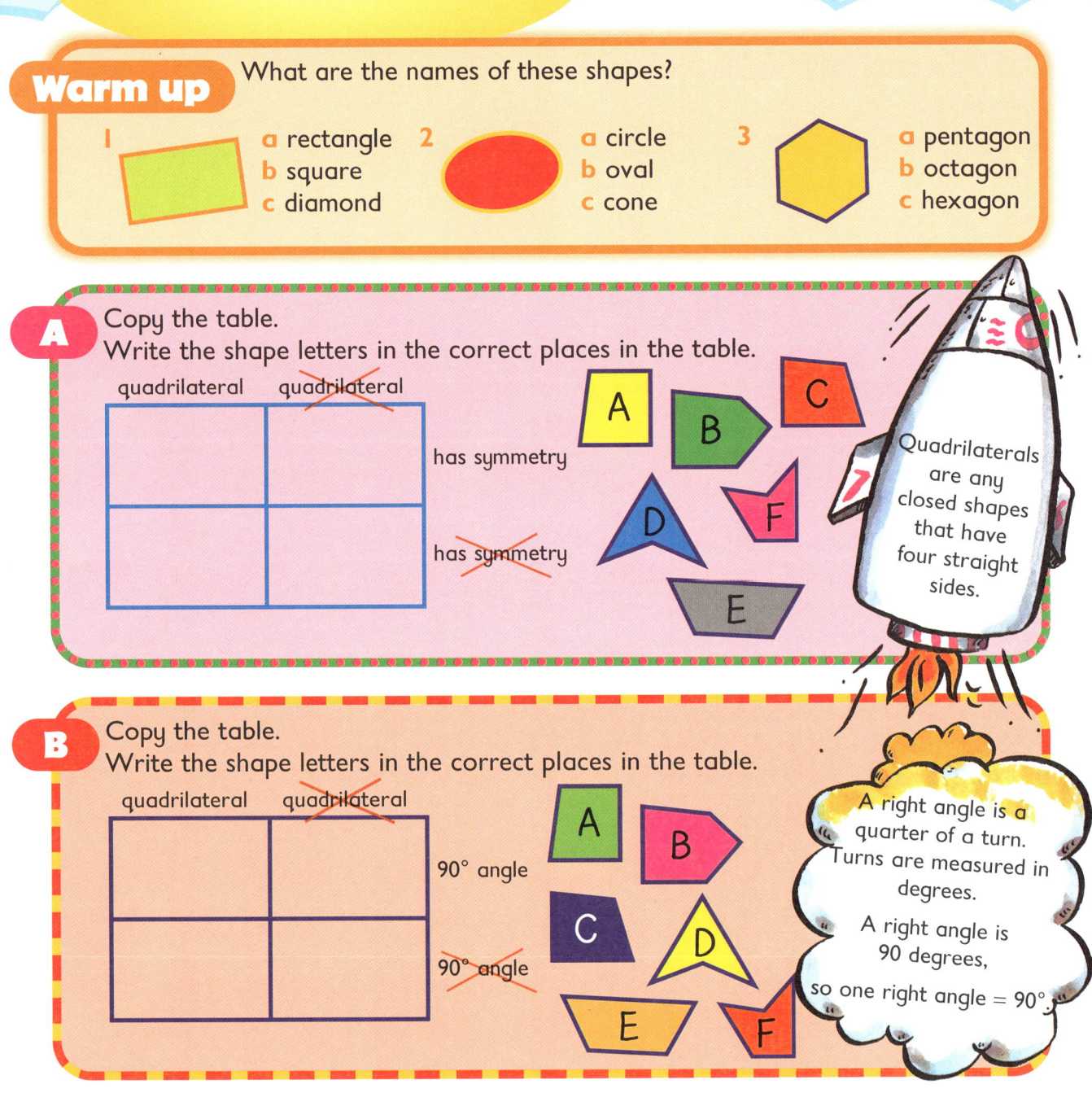

Warm up What are the names of these shapes?

1. a rectangle
   b square
   c diamond

2. a circle
   b oval
   c cone

3. a pentagon
   b octagon
   c hexagon

A
Copy the table.
Write the shape letters in the correct places in the table.

	quadrilateral	~~quadrilateral~~
has symmetry		
~~has symmetry~~		

Quadrilaterals are any closed shapes that have four straight sides.

B
Copy the table.
Write the shape letters in the correct places in the table.

	quadrilateral	~~quadrilateral~~
90° angle		
~~90° angle~~		

A right angle is a quarter of a turn. Turns are measured in degrees.

A right angle is 90 degrees, so one right angle = 90°.

C
Draw this quadrilateral on squared paper. Draw what it looks like after a 90° turn in a clockwise direction.

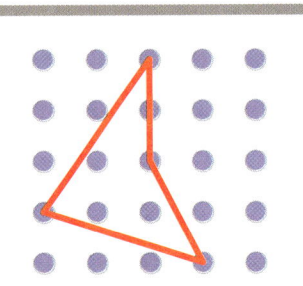

Shape knowledge 2

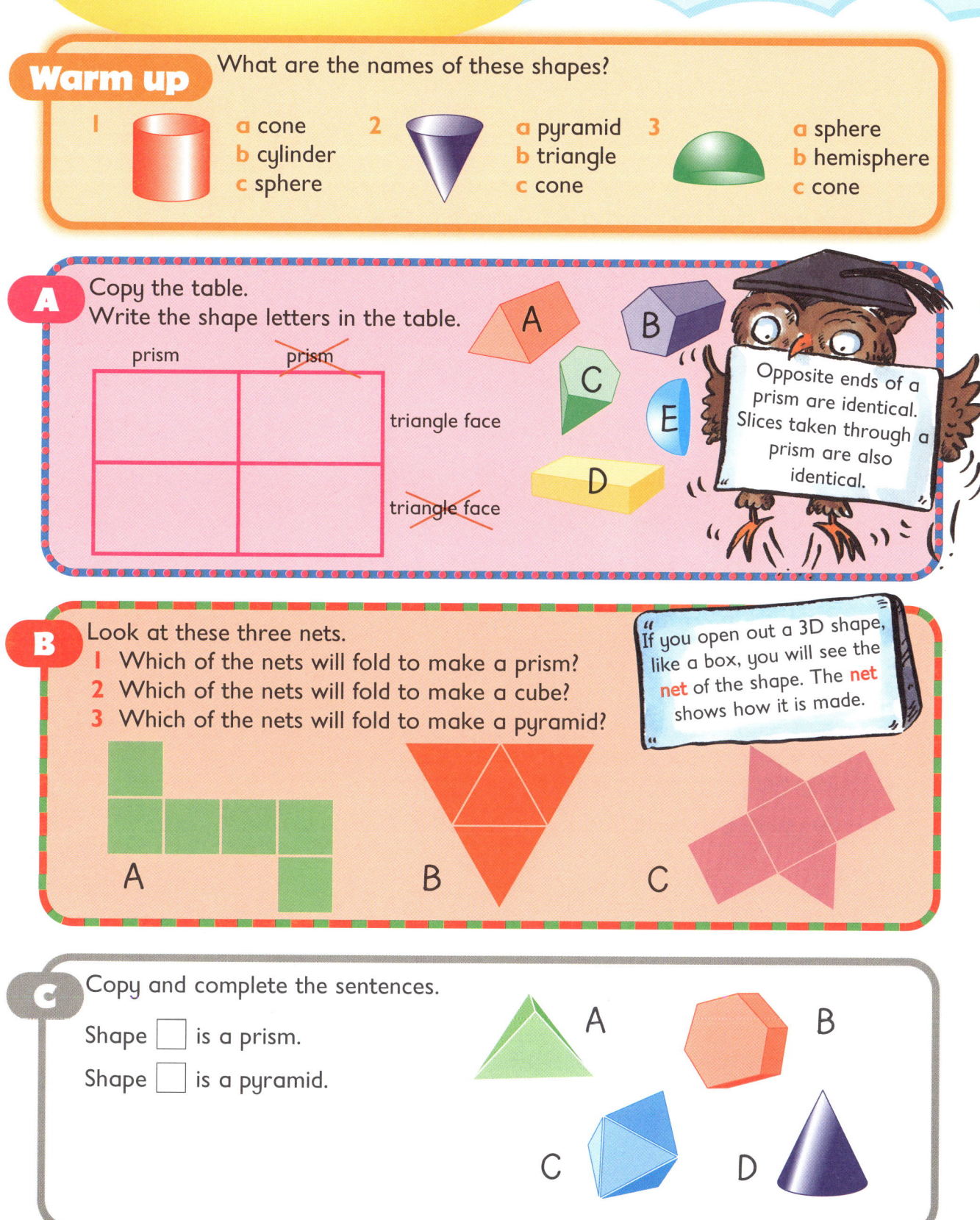

Warm up What are the names of these shapes?

1. a cone
   b cylinder
   c sphere

2. a pyramid
   b triangle
   c cone

3. a sphere
   b hemisphere
   c cone

A Copy the table.
Write the shape letters in the table.

	prism	prism ✗
triangle face		
triangle face ✗		

Opposite ends of a prism are identical. Slices taken through a prism are also identical.

B Look at these three nets.
1 Which of the nets will fold to make a prism?
2 Which of the nets will fold to make a cube?
3 Which of the nets will fold to make a pyramid?

A   B   C

If you open out a 3D shape, like a box, you will see the **net** of the shape. The **net** shows how it is made.

C Copy and complete the sentences.

Shape ☐ is a prism.
Shape ☐ is a pyramid.

A   B   C   D

47

Brainbox

Write the answers to these problems.
Try to answer each one in your head.
Some questions are quite hard.

1 How many centimetres are in 1 1/2 metres?
2 Which number is 10 more than 3999?
3 What must be added to 450 ml to make 1 l?
4 How many pennies are there altogether in three £1 and three 50p coins?
5 What is the tenth multiple of 11?
6 What is 3/4 of £12?
7 Which number is halfway between 137 and 145?
8 Total 15, 37 and 25.
9 What must be added to 24 minutes to make 1 hour?
10 Decrease 135 by 50.
11 What change will you get from £5 after spending £2.55?
12 What is 800 × 5?
13 Double 190.
14 Find the missing number in ☐ − 35 = 120.
15 What is the difference between 996 and 1003?
16 Subtract 99 from 1330.
17 What is 120 ÷ 2?
18 What is remainder when you divide 1368 by 10?
19 What is half £1.70?
20 Subtract 150 ml from 1/2 litre.

How did you do?
Well done if you scored more than 10.
More than 15 is fantastic!